Live Ugly

Live Ugly

Rebecca Eyrick

RESOURCE *Publications* • Eugene, Oregon

LIVE UGLY

Copyright © 2021 Rebecca Eyrick. All rights reserved. Except for brief quotations in critical publications or reviews, no part of this book may be reproduced in any manner without prior written permission from the publisher. Write: Permissions, Wipf and Stock Publishers, 199 W. 8th Ave., Suite 3, Eugene, OR 97401.

Resource Publications
An Imprint of Wipf and Stock Publishers
199 W. 8th Ave., Suite 3
Eugene, OR 97401

www.wipfandstock.com

PAPERBACK ISBN: 978-1-6667-1598-9
HARDCOVER ISBN: 978-1-6667-1599-6
EBOOK ISBN: 978-1-6667-1600-9

JULY 6, 2021

Dedicated affectionately to all those
whom I call family.

And to all of the beauty in all of the ugly of the world.

Contents

Live Ugly | 1

Living

Becoming a Sun God | 5
Birdsongs | 7
Heavenly | 9
The Grand Opening of Pandora's Box | 11
The Motherland | 13
The Witch Doctor | 14
The First Snow | 16
Wild Love | 17
Olive Branch | 18
I'm Tired of my Love Poems | 19
Voices | 20
5 Steps | 21

Ugly

Mornings in Purgatory | 25
Atlas's Ballad | 27
Unbalanced | 30

Lamentations | 30
New Love | 31
Colors | 32
Sycamore | 33
Homage to my Hometown | 34
Wednesday Mornings | 35
My Favorite Fruit is Pomegranates | 36
Hummingbird | 37
Rose-Colored Glasses | 38
Riverwater | 39
Therapy Sessions Alone at 3 a.m. | 40
Apologies of a High Maintenance Menace | 41
Sundays are for Beggars | 42
Learning How to Fly | 43
The Dream | 44

Live Ugly

The world is starting to seem far too small from the
	window ledge where I sit with my best friend.
From here, I can see into the suburbs where wine
	moms rush their kids to and from soccer practice.
I can see the little neighborhoods of dirty houses
	where my friends tell me to be careful,
But the people there send me away with a "be safe, be
	kind, have a good one."

I can see the chapel where I laid begging for forgive-
	ness last week in a rage.
I can see the walking bridge where I danced to sad
	silky songs with a new friend at 3 a.m.
I can see the house of the boy I fell in love with who
	has since forgotten my name but not my body.
I can see the patch of Forest invisible from the ground,
	peaceful and still.

Below me, hundreds of people coming to and from
	wherever they happen to be.
Apartment buildings smaller than the one I've found
	myself in now.
A girl with straightened hair finishing a school
	project.
A boy just waking up from the adventures of last
	night, it's a Tuesday.

I look beside me and I see my friend, skin tan and
    shining in the sun.
A coffee table of half-finished papers and a plate of
    chips and salsa.
Everybody around us waking up in shifts, stumbling
    to get showers and food.
There's something beautiful in the mess here, calm
    and full.

My friend tells me the only place left to look is inside
    myself.
But introspection has proven to hit me where it hurts.
Maybe I'll try to slither out of the muck that's covered
    what I used to love.
Lately I've felt a mess but forgotten how to Live Ugly.

Living

Becoming a Sun God

My skin always darkens in the summer
On days too long spent spinning and jumping it burns
The sun is a great and angry thing.

I used to barter with it for another hour out
My ancestors did the same, for them it was to reap
    another harvest,
I simply want another beam of sunlight to dance in.

My legs hit the earth so hard it shakes and breaks,
Rivers bend to my greatest wish.
My friend tells me it's the old gods I've been speaking
    to in the treetops

I've seen days of tar and cement,
Days when neither sun nor moon show their reign.
Days where it's just me and the empty winds

I pieced my bones back together with my own two
    hands,
And used daisy stems for staples,
Sewed my skin tight with butterfly silk.

What was left ripped up of me gaped open for a while.
Oozing with something dark, we prayed it was the
    universes leeching.
Could be so, now they glow like moonlight.

But now I stand before you, commanding your attention.
I chase the Phoenix and beat it to its resting place.
You ask me who I've become, where I went those dark days

I throw my head back and laugh in response
I turn to the sun and you, angry things.
"Look what I've overcome. Do you not envy me?

Birdsongs

I was never much one to listen to birdsongs.
Their beauty was evident but they never need my
 validation
I found them interrupting the wind's words — I found
 them spitting shards into my ears.

I'd rather press my ear to the forest floor and see who's
 coming.
I'd rather a frog's croak in the mist than the calls
 from above. They say the birds could be angels So
 I hunch under treetops, spare my skin from their
 watchful glares.

I heard the geese flying by in the sunset, and, like a
 fool,
I watched them fly by. Like a fool,
I felt the air beneath their wings in my own lungs.

Despite my best efforts I have to stretch my neck and
 look up.

I tried to yell back at the chickadee in an effort to assert dominance.
It came back stronger yet, with a piercing glowing
 shrieking
Chickadee-dee-dee, chickadee-dee-dee-dee.

Despite my best efforts even screams can't drown the songs out.

I sniffed a hickory tree today. I decided to brand my flesh with its branch,
Where a raven's nest sat.
My blood felt cold on my arm.

Despite my best efforts, just one caw from the ravens beak and I'm sprouting wings.

Maybe the birdsongs are angel's choruses after all.
The crow soared beside me today and, without thinking,
I jumped off the cliff's ledge.

Despite my best efforts, I decided to join in on the birdsongs.

Heavenly

I still remember in the early days
Bowing down to God, begging him for a sign.
Dear God, Dear Allah, Dear the Heavenly Cacophony
That resounded within my bones like a reckoning call from the dead;
From my grandmother. Grandmother, who knew what I never could.
Grandmother, have mercy on me in these coming days,
God allow it I'll harvest the world but until then I'll stick to scripture.
    He's been filling my mind with ideas lately.

I aged like a pagan deity:
Turned bitter over time and personified, but I still look out.
Look out to where I came from and where I'll go because
Quite frankly, it's all a divine loop that begins and ends In one humble spot,
But my heart is pulled and pumped by the moon.
So step by step I'll try to remember why I worship,
While we walk under a burning sun and a dormant sky.

Legend has it that it was not Moses that split the sea,
Rather Yaweh and Yeshua bled divinity into the waters that day.

The water I stand in isn't tinted red yet it washed me,
    my grandmother, and everyone else,
And the power it takes to wash blood stains dry is the
    kind that leaves me thirsting,
So I burst from the waters into the sky reaching for a
    heavenly presence
With a determination so fierce it woke Allah and
    Yaweh from their slumber.
So I keep reaching, leaping, yelping across what could
    presumably be eternity.

Or heaven. Or the hollow in my arms when I pray.

The Grand Opening of Pandora's Box

Being King was fun for the time it was, proudly bearing a holy crown of sins and shameful things
Wearing a crimson robe of pride that dripped from sweat and herbal drugs. Soot from a fire
Spread across his face like warpaint, he felt something barbaric crawl up within him.
A girl danced nearby, twirling with the fire like it's combustion depended on her combusting first.
Like a game of chicken and neither really cared who went up in flames, as long as someone burned.

Unraveling came the thread of sanity, unraveling came unholy structure,
Out in the forest they danced to tribal beats that bled from trees,
That poured from the bear's jaws and rose from the river,
River icy and cold coating an innocent passerby in silver pleated clothes
They drank this up, the girl of fumes and the man, disheveled unshaven with wild eyes.

How intriguing what man can become when opened up like a bomb,
Like a threat, like a one-time snap decision with no turning back.
Once he crawls out of a cage, divinely human, the world has changed.

Once they crawl out, they expose the world to the lack of perfection it needs.

Once I crawl out, I am free! I am free! I am free!

The Motherland

Kiss me on the rails of the ship to the motherland,
On the upper hand, I bathe in the misty morn,
To the sound of Angels horns and final breaths,
Of peace and love and eternal rest.

Now the sky is of embers as are our hearts,
I crumble at the gaze of mother earth,
She holds my body aboard the blessed ship,
"Bathe in my beauty, blessed one."

The falling stars filled our glasses,
So now we shine with heavenly light,
Across the horizon we sit out of reach,
Out of mind but never out of sight.

So kiss me still on these rusty rails,
The world, it fails and pales in comparison to you,
We entertain only the gods and Sun,
We entertain only the Motherland.

The Witch Doctor

The wind blows restless in the trees
Like the witch doctor's eyes
That grow with the crescendoing symphonies
Arising vibrant from the ground and the sky like prayers.

She dreams prophecies at night
And they carry her along like a steady canoe
Floating in chamomile until it blurs her sight,
Home remedies and herbal teas can't shackle the mind.

The mother just birthed the awaited child,
Swaddling him in cloths that smell of sage to trap the innocence.
But he is young and the world is wild,
Like the witch doctor's smirk at every twitch of the mother's desperate hands.

Eternity seems so careless through a simple glimpse,
A patchwork of colors tied together with an uneven stitch,
Like the hut of the old doctor that caves to the commands from her lips,
Because magic isn't magic without the nonchalance.

The ways of humanity are notoriously sloppy,
Like the matted hair and yellowed nails of the doctor,

But she knows her weeds and jars her Poppy,
She mixes her greens and collects her crystals.

The world turns ever to the rising sun,
But truer things come out in darkness,
As the witch doctor inhales and silences everyone
With a smile, a laugh, a holy crooked finger to cover
    her mouth.

The First Snow

I always fall in love after the first snow.
I think my brain recognizes my eventual relapse,
Winter is cold and cruel and has an Icicle Heart.
I try, fruitlessly, to give it CPR, offer a transfusion.

But loving a boy won't summon spring.
I'll have to wait for God herself to send the sun.
Instead I'll lie in a field with a warm heart,
Snow freezing still eyelids once fluttering and lips
   once plush.

There's something peaceful here.
Spine, practically pleated into the earth.
A fox comes to ask if I saw what direction the wind
   went.
I respond only in a gentle exhale, a tired sigh.

I promise the snow only stings for a second.
Come lay with me, let me show you, let me hold you
   here.

Wild Love

Where do the wild things grow, my love?
Where is the starfall that fills up your eyes?
Where Shiva sighs in beauty but dreamt of,
Where your spirit is healed from sacred lies.

You walked from there one glorious morn,
Butterfly wings and lilac dreams follow,
You went to face inevitable scorn,
Shoulders back with the might of Apollo.

So now you've been beaten and broken down,
And the world expects you to turn right back,
But on your head is the wonderous crown,
Of love and might and merciful prozac.

Your eyes melt mercy in the setting sun,
You love yourself endlessly, mighty one.

Olive Branch

I just want to exist as the willow branch.
I always knew I'd need to bend with the wind.
I tend to pray for stronger gusts each time
Praying the world will bend around me too.
Yet oaks stand firm and pines are mighty.
So I will bend and dance for the universe.
Watch me twirl and break like the sea.
I call to the river and it responds with a dove
With an olive branch in its beak.
The sight makes me bray because, finally,
The world might go my way.

I'm Tired of my Love Poems

I'm tired of imagining love in hues of anguish.
Don't let me inhale you like nicotine,
Let me gulp you down like fresh honey.
Wash you down with a lemonade smile and sunlight.

I don't have to make my life a tragedy,
With bruises and fire marking where I've touched.
It doesn't have to be a viral hit.
My pain shouldn't make me more loveable.

I want a love that feels like acoustic guitars
And vials full of peony petals.
I want it to feel like a summer day before rain hits.
I want it to glide. I want it to settle like dust.

Dust. They way it falls when the whole world is still.
And you hardly breathe to watch it fall.
But the exhale won't affect the world's trajectory,
Neither will a rabbit's foot, Or rosemary.

I want my love to seep into my skin.
I want it yellow. I want it fresh. I want it full.

Voices

It's funny how everything changes in an exhale.
The friction of some vocal chords.
It doesn't have to be dressed up and pretty.
Even bagpipes, dismal and aching,
sound beautiful in Irish Misty Mornings.
I don't ask for much, nothing loud.
Just a whisper,
A murmur under a Juniper tree
Saying all things change with time,
A laugh that drips with honey
And falls on the ground and my ears with
The same sticky sense of warmth.
Something warm.
Something full.
Even if it takes years to wash the scent off.

5 Steps

My therapist tells me when I'm shaking
Startled and ready to run,
To find what brings me comfort
The idea is so foreign to me that I struggle with words

5 things to see. An ancient elm tree.
Pictures of the ones I love.
Rain clouds and wooden steps.
Mountains above the sea.

4 things to touch, yarn from my Nana's basket.
The warmest blanket I can find.
The warm skin on my shoulders, olive and clear.
The smooth rock my sister and I found when we were
    young.

3 things to hear, with this one I struggle.
I desire to hear only holy dissonance;
I can only hear them in the wind,
In babies laughter and harmonious choirs from a
    distant room.

2 things to smell,
I prefer lavender and lilac,
But I'd settle also for the smell of wet earth,
Or for the perfume my mother wore when I was
    young.

And 1 thing to taste.
My own saliva doesn't count.
Mint works best, or saltwater of the sea.
Nothing sweet, just what reminds me of life.

Just what reminds me to be alive.

Ugly

Mornings in Purgatory

How do I document dying?
I could slur my words here.
Iwokeupeverydayhopingthatlwouldn't.
I promised God I'd turn holy with time,
But time stops existing when your eyes burn,
Red and itching, it's been a *week*, sleep.
I forgot what mornings were supposed to be,
I spent the early hours mourning who I'd become,
Only to spit when I worshiped sunrise.
I was weak.
The days were a fuzzy blur, all except that sunrise.
Night times spent literally dancing on bridges-
I never jumped though the trains begged for me.

My life was hues of gray, smoke-filled,
Skin dull and hair falling,
But they glowed in mornings.
I was battered in the morning, horny in the morning,
Placing bets on who I'd see that night,
Which body bag would come lay next to mine.
I knew when I'd moan it would sound guttural,
A glimpse of the Rot that built within me each night,
They'd know to run then,
I made love with the nights, never sleeping
For fear the next day would be the same.
God damn, each day was the same.
Day in and day out, prayers
Falling on ears that couldn't hear me.

Let me be clear: my voicebox had faltered,
And my thoughts took a shortcut to the Divine Landfill.
I came to embody this place.
Holy waste hoisted on my shoulders.
Everything was gray and blue.
I tried to travel off the beaten path, take the country roads,
To death, a slow burn, crinkling on the edges.
My hope was upheld by a string,
Held by people playing damage control,
Playing tag to take the pain and let me rest.
I shouldered it for them anyway.

Even now I wonder where this pain went,
Who's hoisting the burdens these days.
Still, change never came when I begged it to.
Not when the old man at the park passed pleasantries,
When I paraded my pain and pounded my pride.
Still, I was dying.
How do I explain this?
Besides an aching sunrise, an empty prayer, deflated lungs?
A choked labido released to the wind?
A colorless landscape?
Every inch on edge, exhaling tired fumes.
Talk to me of pain, I'll be your oracle.
Though I survived, though I lived to sleep through the night,
Mornings then were nothing short of Purgatory.

Atlas's Ballad

Failure is subjective,
I entered life heaving passion
And exhaling
        Desperation for a better —
    The Best — tomorrow.

Wide eyed, I shake like a ticking time bomb,
Until I burst into the world like Icarus daring the sun
To melt me. But the sun is omnipotent and so
The wax on my back falls
        Down
            Down
                Down to the land
                below me.

Wax-burned girls aren't worshipped as they should be,
So crawling among the majority in constant
    discomfort,
I built a ladder from the ground back up to the rest,
        The Middle,
Not quite at the sun but they say I'm where I should
    be.

I work through day in and day out,
And my lungs no longer pulse but marinate in
    molasses.
I'm building a ladder up to nothing, to ideals, to a title
And the irony comes in being closer to

                              God
                    When
               I
       Fell.

But now I'm farther than I've ever been
From truth and transparency. It took me years to
   cover the wax
In powder and petty smiles and gloves on my
   shoulders,
I've fallen defenseless, yet they yell "win,
                                    win,
                                          win!"

Unbalanced

I was born with a throwing knife
Wedged between my toes.
A gift from God for self-defense,
But it spent its days chopping up phalanges
In exchange for a story to tell.
Because of this I learned to walk unbalanced.
A casual walk for everyone around me.
To me it feels like walking a tightrope on a windy day.
I do try, I do.
But lately I've been letting the wind have its way.
The people around me gasp when I fall
Like it wasn't prophesied, like it's not an omen.
I think sometimes I prefer to feel a whirlwind.
I think I'm stuck in it. I think I'm stuck.

Lamentations

How bizarre it is to know how to lament.
At night I dream only of such liberties.
To bang my chest and bawl, to scream, to shudder.
To begin ripping the world apart in handfuls of dirt.
You may do these things; I will sit breathing in the
    mound of earth you threw.

I only recently remembered to breathe, shirt soaked-
    with rainwater.
My lamentations are silent but at least I heal like
    thunder.
At least you know I'm there.
At least bullfrogs and locusts worship my presence.
And so do shining streets.

I will settle stilly into the silences
Between others sobs when they gasp for air.
I will brew and keep the days cool and blue-hazed.
I will wrap my loved ones up in honeydew.
Until they drift to sleep.

You tell me to scream but only praises escape my lips.
Even when they're hollow, they're jubilant.
My rage is only evident in the direction of the wind.
So I will blow cooler still
And piece the world back together.

New Love

I can't pretend I didn't think of Apple trees when I met you.
I won't say you slithered you to me, but I will say
One look in your eyes and I knew why Eve took the fruit.
You tell me one look in mine and you know why Adam followed suit.
We attempted to make our sins heavenly at first,
Flossing apple peels from our teeth before bed,
Only calling out when the skies opened up.
When it comes to new love, I could sit in that feeling forever.
That moment before god came down to exile,
Or the moment of breath before the wind gets knocked out of you.
But you never know those moments until they're gone.
Pretty soon, we found ourselves tangled on the bathroom floor,
The savory indulgences of our actions so rich it was sickening.
Why must they gaze at us like that?
How can something so sinful taste so sweet?

Colors

Yesterday I felt red,
Like my favorite lipstick or
My best friends heels
When we harness all the power we possess in our-
 shaking bodies.

But today I feel gray,
Like the skies that cry and the static,
And all I want to eat is egg salad,
Which should warm me up considering it's yellow and
 bright but I'm still cold

Gray like my monologue that never hits
Point-blank, twisted in telephone wires,
My life is running on coals and I sit still,
Running on gray fumes with vibrant aspirations.

I ate my brain and heart today,
Because neither of them seem to work.
They were gray and dull and tasted of waste,
But at the center of each i found a sturdy core: yellow
 and pink and blue and red.

Sycamore

I'm not even sure what time it is anymore,
But the wall in front of me is gray,
And the daytime seeps away like water
Running through my fingers as I desperately grasp.

Outside is the same, and the house's bones will sway,
And the foxes will feast and the ravens say,
    "Nevermore"
Perching in the Sycamore waiting for me to see,
But I saw years ago so I don't bother looking out
    anymore.

I stay inside and I'm the only one awake,
Feeling stale and my body aches and creaks,
Everything is still so it must be the bleak morning
    hours,
From 2-5 when all in our towers we hide.

My mind feels like TV static but up the volume stays,
And daily life plays on repeat like a broken track,
But I hear the future spoken to me like a dying wish,
So listening back is the only choice I have.

The night is daunting and restless and it never ends,
But time bends for just one more day,
And my body will pay but I find solace in the rising
    sun,
Falling on that grand old Sycamore.

Homage to my Hometown

Brick roads on overcast days
Sunsets at 3 p.m.
Barren tree branches
Uneven sidewalks
Small houses that smell of cigarettes
Burger King before basketball games
Long black hoodies year round
Musty beds
School hallways smelling of puberty and sweat
Skateboarding through them
Yellow fluorescents
Muddy pickup trucks
Smokers corner before school
7 am choking down stale food
Screaming on the beach at 1 am
Monster energy and nicotine
Bloodshot eyes in classrooms
Burnt out streetlights
Geese blocking roads
Graffiti and broken glass in alleys
Overgrown grass by a house long abandoned
Inhabited by stray cats seeking warmth
A unified misery
Grind and trauma and grime
And everything that reminds me of being a teenager.

Wednesday Mornings

Overcast and cold/ snow turning noses and fingers red / bottles hanging from my neighbors tree / clinking when the wind blows — man-made wind chimes, what we've used to fill the spaces / spaces bird songs used to fill / spaces where we start to sink.

A dog across the street barks at a crack addict crossing the corner / everyone else follows suit / barking, barking / have some sympathy / let him breathe / let the tap in his head drip-drip-drip / drip until he comes to / people care so much about suffering until it's suffering they can see / my suffering and his aren't sugar candy enough / we'll choke on lemon juice and grapefruit until they are / when a smile makes me drool / tell me if the saliva is savory enough.

At the last moment, a ray of sunlight / oh to bask in that warmth forever / oh to sit restfully again / oh to sigh in relief / my forehead has permanent downward v's on it / they look like the bird drawings, how we learned it as kids / to you I look disgruntled and aged / to me you look the same / I know you know this kind of pain

My Favorite Fruit is Pomegranates

It used to be so discreet. When my loved ones would
 ask I was a rock
To God and myself
I was a pomegranate and my seeds would seep out
 when the juices were suckled into some mouth.

I don't remember much of being a child
But I do remember lullabies to tell me
God always had by back, but as I aged
I found mercy a High Risk Low Reward situation

These days I stick more to blind exuberance
I worry often that my body is my only advantage
And even that hasn't been enough.

But I still let myself fall from the tree
All men look and taste the same
My seeds drop out among what I wish to be
 wildflowers
But could very well be poison ivy

So I wait for God to let the rains wash over me.

Hummingbird

Your charming hum in my darkest hour, Your heart
    was numb and your mind was sour,
But I had nothing left, no pride to defend,
So hummingbird, charm me again.

Charm me in the starless night of guilty rain,
Find the whitest swan, she's easy to blame,
Make sure that she forgets her name,
Leave her on her knees, broken, praying.

Cardinal watchmen hold my gaze,
Willows dance on stormy days,
Singing the unholy praise,
Of Pretty Eyes in a deadly haze.

Until your humming buzzing makes my head explode,
I had to reap what you bitterly sowed,
My body is bruised to the end of time,
A reminder of when my life wasn't mine.

    — I'm so tired of these god damn bruises

Rose-Colored Glasses

I can feel the blood dripping off my tongue.
You told me it would turn to roses if I swallowed.

I saw you through rose-colored glasses in the first place.
I didn't care that your acid tears burned my fingertips.

You uprooted the weeds in yourself
And threw them upstream so we'd collect them

And plant them in our flower beds.
But I can still feel your grime in my nail beds.

You offer your pocket knife to clean them out.
At this point I'd let you harvest fingers for peace.

You had me swallow my pride instead, a mass system failure.
But kid? Thank you for ripping off my rose-colored glasses.

I pray they serve you well against sunbeams
You claim never bother you, even through the burn.

I'll bathe in moonlight to remove your scent.
Howl to the wind for blood well spent.

Riverwater

Who's to say water wasn't meant to kill us?
Quin Shi Huang coated his esophagus in mercury.
Van Ghoh had an affinity for yellow paint.
My friends prefer whisky.

I'd rather lay on the bottom of a river,
Open my mouth and let water fall in.
Wait to see if my belly bursts or I grow forbidden
    fruits.

Even now, each sip tastes more like metal,
Maybe that's why we crave immortality.
Drink what you can, live while you're young.
The liquor's the river, the chaser's the rum.

Therapy Sessions Alone at 3 a.m.

My friends are all I am.
Don't you want more substance?
Maybe if I become something more
I'd become a little less because I'd stop trying to fill something that just isn't there.
I can't help but recall the ocean tides from when I was a kid
More specifically the sand
What do you remember about them?
The wheels are turning and the movement stops
Something
Something
I wish I didn't have to be so low to be so high
Do they bring you joy?
The Pagan taught me about balance and I'm starting to think he's God
Maybe
I set an antelope skull on my windowsill just in case.
Sometimes I fear I'm too much for some people,
Which is ironic since I just absorb the people around me.
You absorb them?
My personality is a copy, cut, paste.
Nobody knows how to love a sponge. Or a Brick Heart.
And lately, at least for me, there's nothing in between.

Apologies of a High Maintenance Menace

I can feel myself slipping every now and then.
I slice open my chest to show everyone my heart,
They respond with concern, with exhaust.
If I could be low-maintenance I would.

But learning to suture myself came with a price.

Unfortunately it's far too easy to get caught up in my bellows.
My waves are fun until you drown.
And you search for that life raft to pull you out,
But I'm still there, rolling, bleeding, bellowing.

Please, please, please bellow with me.

Sundays are for Beggars

Back when sunrise still held meaning
We were awoken at the first crack
My sister and I packed into matching dresses with puffy slips
A bible and a big white bow as pacifiers.

I'd march to the beat of the morning bell in my church socks
Socks that would inevitably turn black from digging for rocks outside.
Before supper and before bed my mother taught me to give thanks.
I always imagined God watching over me in the trees by my window.

My time as I grew was spent trying to prove my own reverence
My mother spoke me to sleep with bible stories
She'd paint my fingers and toes pink, I'd gulp it all down,
Hold it turning over in my belly until Sunday morning.

Sing to the altar dressed in pink like me.
Even then, atonement was a bargaining game.
I spent years after this painting my nails magenta.
Maybe this sunday I'll try a softer shade of pink.

God, if I do, am I again favorable in your eyes?

Learning How to Fly

I used to look at birds so adoringly.
In a way, I learned to fly before I walked.
I, too, wished to be suspended by nothing,
I wanted to be gone when morning knocked.

I wish I knew I was in the air when I was.
I remember it felt just like falling.
The wind currents stung bloodshot eyes and chapped lips.
Turns out I was never meant to fly.

The Dream

I've been haunted by this dream each night:
A woman, large and disgruntled,
Sitting in an old bathtub,
Some bird on her shoulder.
Around her, the darkness settles.
She comes to me each night, this woman.
  The tub,
    The bird.

Proud and sad all at the same time.
I beg her to speak, to breathe.
I assume she's drowning — the tub.
I assume she's death -
  The darkness, still.
But I know she's beautiful.
I know she has power
  The bird then caws.
I startle at the sound,
I know it means to beckon me forward.
The woman looks godly now,
Something terrifying and alive in her eyes.
I reach out. To the woman,
  The tub,
    The bird.

I startle awake with this feeling in my bones,

Like I saw a beauty greater than could be found on
   this earth.
I have learned to bow now. To grovel before the
   woman.
       The tub,
               The bird.

www.ingramcontent.com/pod-product-compliance
Lightning Source LLC
Chambersburg PA
CBHW072037060426
42449CB00010BA/2319